We Use Tools

Written by Cass Stricker
Illustrated by Phil Parks

Scott Foresman

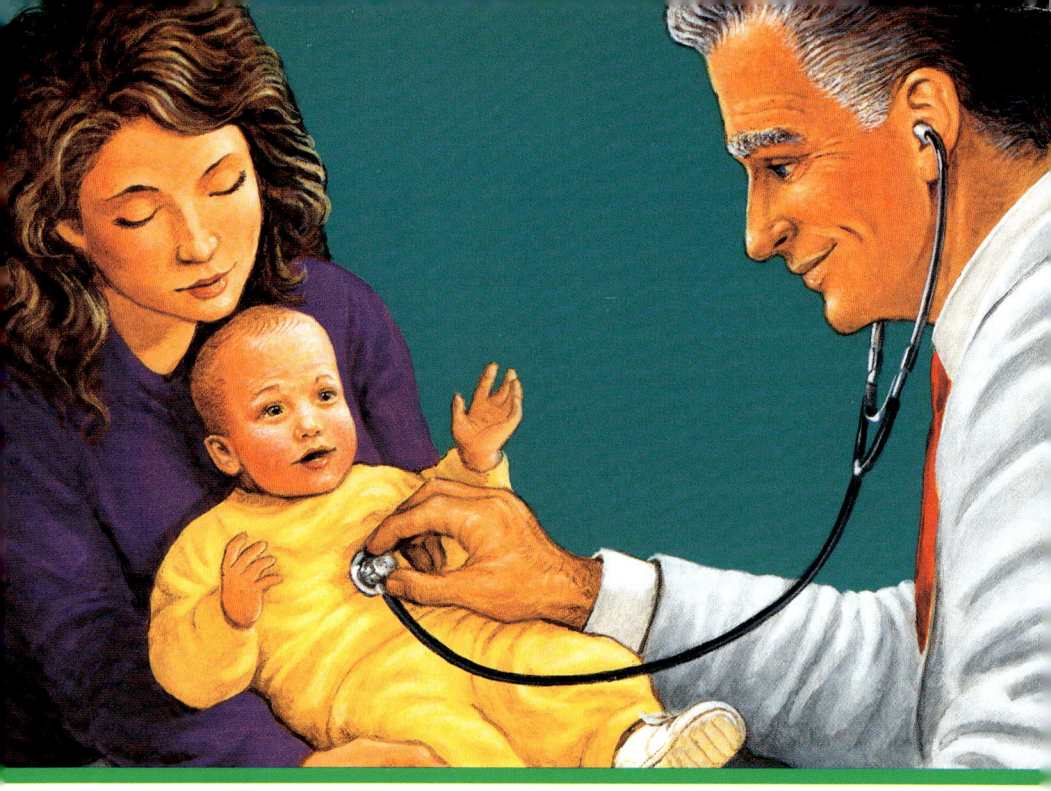

Tools can be quiet.

The man has a tool.

It is a quiet tool.

Tools can be loud.

Can you see a loud tool?

This man has a tool.

It is little.

Tools can be big.

That ladder is a big tool.

Tools can go down.

Here is one.

See it go down.

Tools can go up.

Here is one.

See it go up.

Do you have tools at school?

Do you have tools at home?

We all use tools.